veiled EXISTENCE

a scattering of thoughts on living in turmoil

poetry by Denae Turner

VEILED EXISTENCE

First Printing: 2018
ALANNA RUSNAK PUBLISHING

ISBN 13: 978-1-7752792-5-9
ISBN 10: 1775279251
Alanna Rusnak Publishing
282906 Normanby/Bentinck Townline
Durham, Ontario, Canada, N0G 1R0
www.publishing.alannarusnak.com

Contact the publisher for Library and Archives Canada catalogue information.

Cover photography by Velizar Ivanov, courtesy of pixabay.com
Cover design by Alanna Rusnak

To all those who suffer silently in a broken mental health system through long wait-times, the unavailability of dedicated, knowledgeable professionals, and the exhausting travel to access a big city centre, where specialists are clustered.

May we all be treated with dignity and priority, and may those who suffer from mental illness be given the same concern and consideration as someone who suffers from a physical illness.

Contents

Forward

This collection was written at a time in life where living and breathing became too much to handle. Existing was a full-time job, and I found myself staring at roadblock after roadblock on my journey to find the help I needed. Support for those suffering from mental health issues is seriously lacking, and I found myself the victim of an inept system.

Even though writing was cathartic and important, I wasn't strong or brave enough to see myself as a whole person. Referring to myself as 'i' rather than 'I' signifies deep feelings of unimportance, the loneliness I felt as I faced my illness without appropriate support, and the experience of having a voice that went from small to inaudible. Ongoing stigma forced me into invisibility as I tried to hide the guilt and shame of my illness. I lost myself.

Living my life beneath the cruelty of verbal, emotional, and physical abuse with sexual interference almost broke the whole person I was. *Veiled Existence* contains clear and brutally honest descriptions filled with much darkness and despair, sadness and truth.* This written work helped me release years of inner turmoil, frustration and despair, as I searched within the madness of a broken system, looking for help and guidance.

Had proper systems been in place, this collection may not exist. Birthed out of my anger and frustration, the writing was, at times, the only thing that kept me alive. It is my hope that anyone finding themselves in a similar situation would read my words and find some peace in knowing they are not alone. Reading of my past pains will not rid anyone of their own, but it may light a spark. The system is broken, but I am no longer invisible. If my story moves one person to speak up for change, then everything I've been through is worth it.

The identities, names, and places are not listed and remain anonymous. The name 'Denae Turner' is a pen name derived from parts of the letters of direct family names.

trigger warning, some pieces contain mention of suicidal tendencies and self-harm

VEILED EXISTENCE
a scattering of thoughts on living in turmoil

Denae Turner

2018

tiny little voice

a tiny little voice
that's all there is
nothing left
nothing more...
this tiny little voice
can't be heard
no one has listened
no one has believed...
a faint sound
delicate and soft
struggles for recognition
for acceptance
for belief...

a tiny little voice
always asking
desperately wanting
searching and hoping...
please hear me
and what i have to say...
no matter how strong
how forceful or weak
this tiny voice deserves
the right
as everyone else
to speak the truth
and have the chance
for all to listen
and to hear...

let the tiny voice sound
believe and support
the truth she speaks...
humbled and weak
gentle and small
this right
is her's
just as it is yours...

thinking about
all the wasted years
the moments
the pills...
and all for what?

a field

atop a hill
looking down in a valley
there's a field
where the wildflowers bloom
and the grass
grows long,
the sunshine's bright
the warmth is all around...

gentle warm breezes
lavender and rose
wafting through the air
a picture of silence
of beauty and calm,
the wildflowers grow
the field full of colour
bring little yellow-heads
swaying back and forth

the dandelion
the plainest of them all
it lives
it multiplies
and it never ever dies...
its little tiny secret
when it goes to seed
it trades the head of yellow
for a fluffy crown of white...
the gentle breathing winds

blowing every little seed
scattering, wandering
never ever knowing
a final resting place...

a tiny dandelion
a mere obnoxious weed
resembles all too closely
it parallels my life...
the harsh wind blowing
releasing, scattering
letting go,
one by one
the seeds now drifting
plucked
and without control...
one by one
just like my life
each a fragment
taken from me quickly
everything important
one by one released
the losses insurmountable
stripped bare of most existence
a stem now only left...

atop the hill
looking down in that field
i see my life before me

shattered dreams
scattered thoughts
purpose unknown...

i trusted - what a mistake i made

you alone
walk the road
you alone
carry the load

rely on yourself
let no one in
trust no one
and you
will see
how easy
life will be...

to live each day
as best you can
close the door
and say, "No More!"

shut out the light
and hide from sight...

calm and in darkness
regret and regress
fantasy and fairytales
a life safe
from all harm,
left all alone
to imagine,
pretend...

this is how
i will live
for now
until the end...

purpose?

wounded
deadened
diseased
and broken
life in darkness
all around
no joy
nor pleasure
they can't be found
just torment
more struggle
the journey all mine...

a breath of life
so hard to fathom
inconsolable thoughts
of strife
inner hatred
for all mankind,
God's wondrous
and precious beings
flawed and evil
full of harm...
a heart that's broken
crushed and lifeless
a being tired and worn
what more is there to live for?
what purpose to exist?

tired

deep exhaustion has set in
yet sound sleep
it can't be found...
my body is tired
my thoughts in disarray
and constant crying
gets in the way...
the darkness of night
dreading sleep and its horror
the dreams and the fright
the struggle and fight
the ravages
and battle
as the shroud descends
and the fog circles round
the circle of illness
once more transcends
into the depths of despair
and i'm just so tired
i really don't care...

laughter

ripping wallpaper off a wall
the mess
the filth
and the magnitude of it all
tired and worn
angered
full of rage
emotions unleashed
but no crying or tears
something new
now bursting forth
uncontrollable laughter
deep gut-wrenching
tummy hurting pain...

laughter through anger
through pain and harsh words
through judgement and sadness
abuse and neglect...
my body, my mind, shutting down to it all
heart and mind hardened
nothing left
to break my fall...

the tears have dried up
the pain deadened inside
there is nothing left
except to laugh
i can't cry anymore

pathetic human being
laugh at yourself
laugh at the words
as they come hurtling by
laugh at the curses
the words and abuse
laugh at your whole being
your life
it's a joke...

keep chuckling at life
and the way you've been treated
by puppets and animators
and scene-stealers of strife...
a new way of coping
because the well has dried up
it all started so suddenly
and without any cause...
i can't take my life anymore
and so i want to change
but no one is there
and never will be...

trapped inside

trapped inside
this aged body
a tiny little girl
awaits...

trapped inside
and hidden
from view
a tiny little girl
she lives...

trapped inside
her cries
the tears silenced
throughout
the years...

trapped inside
with nowhere to go
and no way out
the fight begins
once more...

trapped inside
there isn't much room
for her
and the other
to live...

who is stronger?
who will win?
who will stay inside?
who gets out
to face the world?
to tackle the pain
the truth
and lies...
the struggle
just to survive...

trapped inside
the girl wants out
'Daddy, Daddy,
please
just hold me'
'Mommy mommy
hug and kiss me,
tell me that you love me'...
'come and get me
dry up all my tears,
please don't leave me
hold my hand real tight'
Can you hear me?
Daddy?
Mommy?
where oh where are you?

trapped inside
no sound is heard
little girl's alone
once more...
the other
the aged
has shut her up
with force
and anger now...
determined to reign
and show who's boss
the other
won't let her out...

the two
continue
to live each day
trapped inside
the shell...
living together
sharing the being
with no way out
for either...
forever trapped
and living in bondage
survival is for the fittest...
who will wither
and who will prosper?
time will only tell...

purpose unknown

my lot in this life
has been filled with turmoil
sadness and death...
the cloud attached
to the soul
darkness all around
consumed and oppressed
wandering
life without purpose
desire or want...
the question to be asked
why?

why has this happened
a human
a lifetime of struggle
trying to breathe
wanting to live
forever searching
for the elusive prize

PEACE...
where did it go?
maybe i never had it...
maybe that too
is all an illusion
my mind
a mixed up bag
of dismantled dreams

black and white pictures
and fuzzy memories
that become fainter
with each passing day...

where is this PEACE
that everyone wants
that everyone seeks?
can anyone tell me?
tired of wandering
of searching
and looking...

life is filled
with nothing anymore
the 'peace' i never ever had
the body is tired
the mind is exhausted
and the word 'hope'
permanently erased
from my vocabulary...
the body
the mind
to be whole
a wish not made
to become true...
giving up
and running away
sounds so easy to do...

one by one

everything is taken away from me
the important things
the important people
all backing away
ridding themselves of
my disgust
the troubled and mixed-up mind
ever so quiet
so that maybe
being screwed up
in mind, body, and soul
i won't actually see
that i am being tossed aside again
used once more
played with like a toy
and this filled with boredom
discarded and left alone...

the soul is now empty
the heart is hard as stone
and the meaning and purpose
of my life
is now the question of the day...
how much more can i really take?
how much more our life's events
will kill my inner being?

one after the other
like strokes from the whip
the pain they inflict
breaking down my spirit

my being
and my life...
what is going to happen
when i fall
and can't get up?
too weak to carry on
to be alive
and so near to death...

i am of no good to anyone anymore...

the game for the sick

just take one more
just try this one
we'll add an increase next time
need a refill?
quite a collection
i now possess...
little trophies of success
the way to winning it all...
you haven't helped me
at all...

i have possessed
the demons
that infected my father's mind...
i am the product of
everyone else's desires...
and you see,
there is no real cure
pills, capsules, tablets
all in lovely colours
cheap talk, empty promises
a trail of paperwork
so long...

the system
too broken to care
constant mistakes
covered and hid
the eyes never finding

the ears never hearing
the truth
the diagnosis
if there is one

keep feeding
the mentally ill mind
the worn and tired body
at the end
of their ropes
vulnerable for care
downtrodden in life
keep them sedated
deadened mind and thought
expressionless
emotionless...

too many drugs
too many saviours
too many power gods
all with their own agendas

—when do you finally say
enough is enough?

what life has become

value
purpose
meaning
love

wishes
feverishly wanted
and never granted

words spoken
have no meaning
lacking in truth
emotion and will
the eyes
now
only see
the colour grey...

the hurt
the anger
the sadness
all hidden deeply within

beautiful lovely eyes
that once shone brightly
laughed with the wind
and breathed in life
embracing its beauty
revelling in the masterpiece

to be alive
to experience
to feel...

somewhere
somehow
life has changed...
disappointments and events
piled too high
they came too fast
to breathe
to live
and try to survive

the struggle
it carries on
each day
more difficult
than the last...

belief in hope
in existence
to find the pureness of joy
the missing elements
in a life
that has gone horrible wrong...

where are they?
the kind
the caring
the gentle

where are they?
in the depths of despair
in my brokenness
i continue to search
but not one
is worthy
to come forward
to take notice
of the pain
and the hurt
that flows inside...

to whom do i
entrust my thoughts?
my inner self?
the conflict
that lies within?
to whom
do i share the agony
of my life?
the people who
inhabit this earth
have and continue to
take my hope
my existence
my purpose
so that
i believe in no one
not even myself anymore

it has become

it has become
a life filled with fear
it has become
a life violated
of safety
it has become
a life betrayed of trust
it has become
a life filled with emotion
overwhelmed
by grief
terror
horror
rage
despair
it has become
a life
filled with
tremendous loss
and sadly
this is MY life

you never asked

YOU
you walked through the door
and sat right down
never once asking
how i was…
a business-like attitude
not caring to ask
to find out
to delve inside
my troubled mind
you never once asked…

YOU
i look up to
i thought you cared…

YOU
have shut me out
like all of the others
a blackness i see
your eyes
they behold the truth
coldness
lack of concern
compassion
and trust
you never once asked…

YOU

i see clearly
that YOU cannot help me
you never did
and never will...
a pretence
an act
fake
like all of the others...
i tried to tell you
but YOU
and the whole world now
don't seem to care...
WHY?
it is your job
your profession in life
to care
to look after...
how come YOU
never once asked?

let me tell YOU why...

YOU are tired of me
my baggage is too much
YOU can't penetrate
the fortress within
YOU don't know how...
years and years
they continue to pass
the system
it fails

the help
not readily available
waiting
and wondering
what comes next...
and what do i do?

YOU are a fake

YOU are nothing

and i am
sick to my stomach
thinking about
all the wasted years
and all for what?

YOU are like the others
what YOU have done
is no different from them...

YOU too
sadly
have let me down
abandoned me...
how come YOU never once asked?

you are flawed too

my strength
it came from you...
the courage to live
to try once more
all from you...
i learned
all over again
how to believe in me...
you took me
into deep crevices
hidden from truth
prying the door open
you showed me
a self worthy of love
a gentle woman
needing warmth, love
and affection...

You showed me reality
the way it is now
black and white
acceptance
forgiveness
time to move forward
i depended on You
your strength
your courage
your kindness towards me...
i put You on a pedestal

unfair i now realize...
for You are not perfect...
i won't listen
to your past

Schizophrenia...
NO!!

How can i trust you?
How can i open up to you?
Professionally
i am terrified now
wondering if i have
a physician
capable of doing his job
being there in one whole being
and if this is all a dream to him...
NO!

Empty i sit
looking for answers
depressed from crying

You are flawed
like i am...

You are NOT perfect
and never will...

you are human
disappointed and scared

i feel used and cheap
lonely and down...
i relied on a person
i thought i knew...
i enjoyed our talks
our friendship
the wise words
of wisdom
truth
and reality...

this is what i want

to have strength of character
that is what i want...
to make decisions
to think clearly
to be on top of everyday events
to share a warm hug
to wear a smile instead of a frown
this is what i want...

to have the courage
to forge ahead
to set some goals
and go after them...
to rid the fear
the anxiety
the thoughts of failure
to stand tall and proud
and walk with determination
this is what i want...

to know my true self
and rid the inner turmoil
that has consumed me
for so long...
to be set on a path
without bends or turns
to be whole once more
this is what i want...

to know what my purpose
in life is to be
i don't seem to have found it
as of yet...
to feel important
to me
and to others
to be valued and treasured
loved and admired
for the person i am
for the person i have become...
this is what i want...

a fantasy
my life has become
distorted views
of love
marriage
self-worth
my value to others
to my family and friends
i am drifting once more
away from what is real...
frightened where this path
will lead me
with jumbled thoughts
of what to do
where to go...
too many voices
i can't seem to be rid of them
quiet rest

it brings me solace
peace from turmoil
and distress...

retreat then
to a world of quiet...
gentle dreams
gentle breezes
deep calm breathing
so peaceful

sometimes
i don't want to wake up...

a time that is past: a remembrance

quietly i awake
everyone else
deep in the land
of peaceful slumber...

August 11, 1990
a day forever etched
filled with excruciating pain
numbness
sadness
despair
the pain so intense
so consuming...
never felt before

a memory filled with tears
a heart forever broken
a happy content life
forever left behind...

a decade now has passed
where has the time gone?
have i lived
in a fog
a blur
for ten years?
i have no memory
of the years that i've lost...
my children growing up

vacations, happy times
my husband and his needs
his wants
his desires
his accomplishments
his achievements...

my Mother is gone
i must learn to say this
MY Mother is Dead...
i am a motherless daughter
it has taken me a decade to recognize this
the pain
still raw
emotions forever numbed
my life a waste
having lived in the past
trying to bring back
a life that once was...

though physically not here
she is not dead
she is alive...
look into the eyes
of her children
her son and daughter...
and look into the eyes
of her four grandchildren
that is where
my Mother now lives
strong and vibrant

full of love...

the past
i have forgiven
no need to look back
ever again...
time has not taken away
the pain...
the memory now dulled
i must open my eyes
look clearly ahead
to MY life...
and leave you gently behind...
yes Mother
i need to do this...
you would want me to do this
this i DO know
So on this anniversary
Mother — i need to close a chapter
the one that contains You and i...
and i must try
with all of my strength
to do this final act...
we WILL meet again Mother
of that i am sure...
hold a place for your daughter
right beside you
if you will
reserve a spot
just for me
and until that day

i will try to live passionately
full of life
full of hope...

i must now say these words, Mother
the words that
are so filled with tears
Goodbye...
just for now
i must
i need
to move forward
with my own life now...
i DO love you
and i always will

is this all a dream?

i sit back and wonder
is this all a dream?
have i been living this
or is it make-believe?
sometimes i float
outside my body
watching it all
taking it all in
wondering if this year
is real or surreal
it must be
a dream
this really didn't happen to me
why did i let this
take over
control me
weaken me
ruin me

what have i done?
i have ruined the being
that i was once proud of
i long for my confidence
the strength
the ability
to handle everyday moments
without feeling anxious
without feeling panic
and having to reach

for a pill
this all must be a dream...

did i dream that i would
actually try to take my life?
did i dream that i wanted to die
and give up?
did i really think that
spending money could get rid
of this?

get me out of my dream!
this all must be a bad dream...
the crash last week
my whole life
came before me
in that split second...
what i was and what i have become
my children's tears
the pain
the loneliness
their mother not there
or their father as well
eyes opened wide
never to hide
this year was real
and not surreal

i woke up...
this is not a dream
anymore...

it's okay

it's okay...
that i am alone
for most
of the day...
it's okay
that my friends
have all left
and look elsewhere
for fun, good times
and love...
it's okay...
i know life's not fair
it's okay...
that i needed
someone today
to talk to
about my visit...
it's okay...
that no one was there
it's okay...
i am used to this
all of my life
it's okay...
i now stand tall
i don't need anyone
i am cold
and hardened
lacking emotion
it's okay...

always an island
amongst the sea
always giving
never receiving
destiny
so full of pain
disappointment
and loss...
it's okay...
i don't need comfort
i don't need friends
i don't need anyone
to make amends...
i don't need a hug
a kind gentle word
for it's been too long
haven't felt for awhile
it's okay....
my self-confidence is gone
i've shut off all
that is within
i am strong
i have me...
no one can hurt me
harm me or use me
yes i am alone
my life without friends
but really, don't worry
because...
it's okay...
i have accepted

that this is my life
the tiny little flower
struggling to survive
in the vast desert...
really...it's okay

my little friend...

my little friend's name
is Gabby...
she's orange, hairy
and small
my little friend
is always there
ever so loving
patient and kind
God has given you to me
for a reason
sweet little one
you have far exceeded
your job here
on earth
and throughout all
of my illnesses and
life's ups and down
you were there
loving me...
you didn't judge me
it didn't matter to you
that i had no job
that i was a mess inside
all you wanted was to chance
at loving mommy
snuggle right up to her
licking her
telling her everything
was going to be okay...

you have become my true companion
what a gift you are
dear little Gabby
and as tears well up
in my eyes
i give thanks this day
to the Master who has given
you another chance
my dear little Pomeranian
Gabby...

i cry...

i cry for me
for my life
and what used to be
for simpler times
that i once more want to see
i cry for my being
my happiness, my dreams
the future it seems
is now fleeing
where are you mom?
i keep wanting to know
why did you have to go?
my heart is broken right in two
it seems no one can fill what you do
your death for me
was the start of my fall
and ever since then
my life had no call
i cry for my life and what used to be
feeling important and confident
all of my strength is now spent
on trying to find the real being ME
i cry for my job
the one that i loved
the pride that i took
from that one little job
i cry for my little dog
who is sick
her heart is so weak

my good little friend
what will i do
when that time... it will come
i will be lost, lonely without you
i cry for what i have missed
since your death dear little mom
someone to hold me, someone to kiss
someone to share
and someone to care
my life now is all, all scattered 'round
no purpose, no meaning
my nerves shaky and wound
tighter and tighter
like i want to explode
i used to be strong
no longer a fighter
i cry for my family
that once used to be
the four of us, mom, dad, and brother
and me...
i cry for the family that i wanted
deep down
a family who loved and wore smiles
and not frowns
that family today
is now only a fragment
a dream... a dream
i am afraid to say
i cry for my life
and what used to be
someone please help me

i seem to be lost...
i want to be happy
and smile once again
it's taking so long
i just wonder oh when
i have been dealt with life's sad events
more than my share
than i can handle
not fair!
i cry for me
my life
and what used to be...

goodbye dear friend

i guess it's time
to say goodbye
i can't handle
the silence
the waiting
wondering where you went
wondering what i did wrong
why you have left
with no notice
no concern
was it too hard
to write a note?
explain the reason
you didn't need me anymore?
was it all really a dream
that you befriended me
in my time of need?
and that i lifted you
up in your time of despair
i miss you more than you will ever know
a lost friend,
a treasure once valued
you have left a void
in my being
so close, so caring
always a kind
and tender word
never a harmful thought
about anyone...

no explanation
just one day
up and gone
leaving those who
cared and worried about you
sad
because
you are not a mean person
you would never hurt
a close friend
is that what we once were?
i miss you
your friendship
your smiles and concern
you are gone
thank you for the gift
that you have given me
you were there for me
when i was most troubled
you befriended me
you gave me your friendship
happiness to you always
dear friend
but it is time to say goodbye...

i know where you have gone...

i know where you have gone
you thought i wouldn't find you
but i did...
one lonely night
searching through rooms
coming across your name
yes, it is you
there is a pit in my tummy
the pit of sadness
the ache
the pain of friendship
i know where you have gone
you thought i wouldn't find you
but i did...
i have wondered
should i make the connection
again?
No
Not this time...
you haven't answered me
so i will watch you from afar
since you have walked away
from me
turned your back
i am somewhat lost
you have moved on
away from this place
but you didn't
tell me why

not one reply
not one goodbye
friends don't do that
maybe we weren't friends
after all...
you must be afraid
to comfort me
that is the reason
for the coldness
the hardness
the lack of concern
i wanted so badly
to tell you
all about things you have missed
but
you are not interested
anymore...
i know where you have gone
but this time
i will only watch
with tears
knowing that you
are responsible for them

brokenhearted
full of sadness
and loss
never ever thought
you would or could do this
to me...
was this all a fake

a façade?
i feel used
you made me feel that way
i trusted you
as you trusted me
you will need strength
in your days ahead
and i will NOT be there
for you have
destroyed
the bond
forever.

dead

DEAD
TOTALLY DEAD
FLATLINE
NO EXISTENCE

NO MEANING
WASTE
LEAVE ME DEAD
WHY DID YOU
BRING ME BACK?

i NEVER WANTED TO COME BACK
i FOUND MY PEACE
YOU TOOK IT AWAY
YOU BROUGHT ME BACK

FLUIDS
CHARCOAL
NEEDLES
I.V'S
PAIN

DEAD WAS BETTER

constant mixed thoughts

there is someone inside
waiting to get out
wanting to scream
wanting to shout...
a bundle of nerves
all tangled up
pressure is mounting
before the explosion
what is the matter?
what am i like this?
what did i do?
am i being punished?
for what i can't
think of...
rage
anger
depression
no emotions
loneliness
memories of childhood
trying to be perfect
always alone
by myself to cope
mental and verbal abuse
not knowing how to love
scared of feelings...
memories of pain
sadness and despair
of so many losses...

can't shake this
it's starting all over again
no self esteem
scared of large crowds
and of seeing people
and leaving the house
opinions of others
i need to ignore
they harm me severely
as they bury deep inside
i wonder if i am worthwhile
or is it true
i am a lazy woman
who does nothing for her man
he has to do everything...
tired of the words
endless and thoughtless
i am screaming
from the inside
something needs to get out...
pent up emotions
memories
feelings
i continue to wander
from day to day
but where is this leading?
i have no direction
no meaning or path
nothing brings joy
contentment or calm
just a jumble of things

without purpose or thought
stuck in a time out
somewhere out there...
i continue to search
for the purpose behind
all the turmoil
the strife
that's been in my life
deep, deep inside
there is someone
who's screaming
for help to get out
that someone is in there
but scared to try
the pain, the emotion
the sadness
too powerful
still waiting
wandering
searching and hoping
for that quietness
peace and serenity
the mind deeply craves...
little person inside
please try to hold me
be patient with me
i am trying to help
you will have your freedom
one day i hope
and then we will
both put this saga

behind us...

invisible figure

a silent voice
a tiny figure
hiding way down deep
looking
waiting
all alone
in a world
that's all her own...

i am here
can't you see me?
why won't you listen?
i stand alone
no one notices
the cries
the hurt
the sadness...

what do i need to do?
hold a gun?
hold a razor?
swallow a handful?
wear a mask?
hold up a flag
of another colour
hoping to get noticed?

what i choose to say
i feel is so important

i try to get involved
included
but no one's there to reply
it's like i'm invisible
not vital or alive
or worth the bother
to give a minute
to make a little smile...

my heart is big
full of kindness
caring
and love...
i stand alone
this is my life...
alone in my own little world...
i try and try
maybe too hard
but it is out of
my desire to have a friend...

there is good in
each and every being here
open up and reach to help
all of those
with fear...
a kindly word
a gentle hug
just knowing that you care
will make a world of difference
if only you would share...

two different faces

tonight you showed me
two different faces...
one so kind
full of caring
and one i didn't recognize...

it was like
you were an actress
fully in disguise...

i didn't seem to know you
you were different
cold
insensitive...
there was no feeling,
emotion
just words upon a screen...

lacking in concern
you didn't seem to notice
the hurt
and disappointment
that made me feel alone...

all too many times
it's happened...
those i've called a friend...
open up to warmth
and friendship...

then just pushed away...

use me
love me
discard me
when you want...

there is always someone better...
i'm always
left...behind

anniversary

Today marks a year
of calling this place home...
one year of love
compassion
friendship
and hope...

Faceless people
words on a screen...
trying to fill
that void
the pain
the loneliness within...

This place is a haven
for those who have fallen...
whose lives have been broken
by certain twists of fate...
an escape from reality
becoming a new identity
black
white
yellow
christian
non-christian...
man
woman
young
old...

come to the meeting place
the central core
to try to get
back a life
once more...

We are all of one cloth
you and i
in this place...
regardless of race
colour or creed...
still searching
for the peace
tranquility and
normalcy
that once was...

So many gifts
i've been given
here...
friendship
and love...
kindness with
compassion...
and all by unknown faces
and words on a screen...

So i humbly thank
all of those who showed
a desire to care
and share their time

with a complete
unknown
faceless
person...
with complex thoughts
and misguided acts
You've helped
and guided me
along my path...
you all were my lifeline
in good times and bad...

Happy Anniversary
one year
here...
still hanging around
much work yet to be done

motherless daughter

i am a motherless daughter
hungry for love
craving that touch
that means so much...

isolated
alone
keeping within
all the torment
and anguish

feelings of pain
abandonment
isolation
i don't belong
my family is gone
i stand out
from the rest...

no little trips
to the mall
for new clothes...
no cozy lunches
or calls on the phone...

no little reminders
or suggestions
about things...
fix your hair

get some colour
you're pale
don't you care?

let's share the recipes
at Christmastime
this year...
you make half
and i make the rest...
what size do the kids wear?
i've found some great sweaters...
i'll buy them for birthdays
if that suits you okay?

the ache
the longing
the nurturing...
i miss to this day...
so many questions
left unanswered...
your past
my identity
fading away...
part of you
your family
i will never ever know...
a mystery
a secret
the unknown history
part of you
i will never know...

i still hold you dear
to my heart
and my soul...
my journey has been rough
long
and i am tired...

i am a motherless daughter
just as you once were
i understand the pain
you felt
as your world ended
like mine...
we share those similarities
the same pain
the same anguish
the same abandonment
of losing a mother
you at twenty-seven
and me at thirty-one...

goodnight
Mother
i am going to rest
i am going to live
my life to the fullest
starting this day
when i awake...
i need to more forward
get on with my life
if by chance i am taken

from this place
i will know that i have lived my life
to the fullest
appreciating all...
the good and the bad...

i am a motherless daughter
for the rest of my life...
i don't want to fight
this fact anymore...
i need my rest now
i will see you again
but for now, Mom
i need to be whole
i need to live...

my father and i

my father and i
we sit in the room
the closeness we feel
we can't express...
silent thoughts
unspoken words
we are two alike
my father and i...

my father and i
we share a bond...
we both put up walls
to keep out the hurt
we are both kind
soft-spoken people...
we share a bond
we look alike...
i am your daughter
dark eyed
dark haired...
stubbornness you gave me
and that quick temper too...
your love of music
instilled
in my youth...
my career
which you desire
from afar...
you gave me everything

i needed
wanted
and sacrificed many things
to give me my future...

my father and i
sit in this room...
the nurturing
tender looks
the maternal caring...
the parental guidance...
it is not there...

you have done your job
as a father and husband...
you sit back gently now
alone in your own world...
the freedom you have
the freedom you enjoy...
this is your time
trips and parties
concerts and movies...
your schedule is full
and doesn't include me
my life has been so dramatically changed...
you aren't my mother
and never will be...
you can't provide the love
the guidance
the concern
i miss so much...

i feel orphaned
like an abandoned child...
always searching
always running...
at seventy-eight your life
is yours
to do with as you wish
you've done your job...
raised the family...
how i wish you were younger
more time on our side...
the clock has started ticking
precious reminders
of memories in the past...
each time i see you
could it be the last?

my father and i
we sit in the room
we both know each other
and the silence
from one another...
just together
alone
no words need to be spoken
my father and i...
my father and i...

little brother

little brother
we stand alone
to face the world
without our mother...
it's you and me
left to cope
left to feel
the hurt
the pain
to deal with
the loss
the abandonment
of not just one
but two...
dad is around
in his own little world
no more nurturing
no more parenting
his part is finished
and we are alone...

little brother
i once despised you
hated you...
because you were mom's boy
her favourite...
no matter how hard i tried
i couldn't break your bond...
you were the preferred male

i was only a girl...
you made my life hell
and hers as well...
the abuse
the tempers
the fighting continued
i had a chance to escape...
i took it
and left...

little brother
i saw you grow up
from a boy
to a man...
i've seen you mature
as a loving man
husband and father...

little brother
i made a promise to mom
the day before she died...
she looking deep and searching
into my tear-filled eyes...
"i am worried about your brother
and how he will cope...
promise me, dear,
that you will always look
out for him
as long as you live"
looking back now
i wondered why she didn't think of me

and who would watch my struggle
my pain
trying to hold
lives together...

little brother
you and i
we stand alone
gaining support
comfort
love...
a closeness shared
by not too many...
we are all we have
our parents no more...
we have put the past
way behind...
no regret
no more anger
no more hatred...
only a dependency
to help each other
nurturing
parenting
love
and kindness...
you give these gifts to me
as i give them back to you with love...

little brother
i have come to

depend on you each day
my little brother
now grown up...
Mom would be smiling...
we are closer than ever...
i love you little brother
we stand tall together
my little brother and i

cold insensitive woman

You don't respect me
i saw that today...
everything i stated
you just looked
the other way...

i am your colleague
didn't you know?
You talked down
to me
belittled me
couldn't you see?

i have an illness
and it is my secret...
You haven't a clue...
i am still productive...
alive...
your equal...
Your eyes are blind
closed from being
self-centred
egotistical
two-faced
and a liar...
a poor excuse
for an administrator...
i once looked up to you
your concern

and interest...
it was an act...
You kept me quiet
that was your goal...
you succeeded there
told me what i needed to hear...
i'm ashamed to call you
my colleague...
we don't share
the same ideals
concerns...
the difference being
that i treat others
with care and respect...
i have a heart
and yours has shrivelled up...

You need to take lessons
go back to school...
learn to be human
that's a good rule...
i AM your equal
on paper alone
the same letters
engraved in the stone...
the road we travel
breaks into a fork...
my path
it leads to love
kindness
compassion to others...

yours...
well...
i will pray for you

dull

it dulls my senses
lessens the pain...
lacking emotion
and dulling my brain...
thoughts so jumbled
memory lacking
a zombie state
at a very slow rate...
tired and sleepy
messy home
cluttered existence
living two lives
completely separate
of each other...
the meds make me quiet
a person looking out
not really involved
in life as before...
a fortress built from pain
surrounds the image
portrayed...
no key
no password
can penetrate the wall...
i love the poor
the needy
the lonely
the sick
those to whom i can show

the real person within
i continue to give
with all of my heart
never wanting to receive
just to give totally
i don't want closeness
too afraid of past hurts...
now
i am a moving
living zombie....
a product of depression
a dependent user of Zoloft
to get through each little moment
each little day
without having a breakdown
or crying spell
that lasts all day...
the robot moves
the mind is dull
productivity ceases
Zoloft is the master
i am the slave...
will i ever get my freedom?
will i ever be in control?
sit and wait...
obey...

time will heal
the mind
the body
the soul

the person within...
the only healer
is the one who believes
i want to be one of those
who can be a believer

a fantasy life

i see my life
as one of fantasy
looking out beyond
the window of truth...
alive and moving
a moment brings
an hour
a day
a year...

what is the truth
of my existence?
is there an answer
to this complex question?
or
do i just keep moving
automatically programmed
to wear the smile
dress the part
wear the makeup
be the mom
be the wife
the music teacher
the friend to all...

but...
where do i fit
into this masked charade?
why am i here

in this place
so far from home?
what am i doing?
why did i leave?
i am lost and confused...
where did the time go?
it has escaped from me
now too late to go back...
what was i thinking?
why couldn't i see
what the future would bring?
i've been asleep
in a fantasy world...
self-centred and oriented
a fight for survival
looking out beyond the glass
not really understanding
my actions
the actions of others
my past decisions
right and wrong...

in my search for perfection
avoidance and freedom
i have lost my being
my sense of belonging...
i don't know me anymore
the course my life has followed
isn't the one i had planned...

my life was such a joy

so full of smiles and laughter...
but somehow it spiralled
downward
never gaining strength to rise once more...
so now i sit and wonder
what my life is worth today
if things that happened
were ever real...

is this just a journey
that is unfinished
a make belief little fantasy
or is this the makings of what
i decided
a course i must finish to the end...
i feel like nothing is real
that deep down i want to go back...
it's like i have been away
on one big holiday...
that's what my life has been
like living out of a suitcase
never knowing
always moving
forever searching...
and for what?
my little fantasy world

swollen eyes

did you notice, Dad
that my eyes were red
all swollen and puffy?
did you know that
you were the cause
of the pain
the grief
my sadness?
far into the dark of night
alone i grieve
for the past
when you used to care
when my being mattered
the tears they flow
each waking moment...
realizing no matter
what i do now
nothing can bring you back
to me...
red swollen eyes
the tears of yesteryear...
the pain forever stabbing
left alone
to deal by myself
to survive without a parent
lacking in love
in kindness
and in caring...
no longer Daddy's little girl

just a part of your past
with the same dark look
yes we're related
somehow i guess...
i feel deserted
unloved
abandoned by you...
if mom only knew
the pain and anguish
the desertion you caused...
abandoned by everyone
lacking in love
there is no one around
i must hold onto myself
i am the only one left...
you continue to hurt me, Dad
you probably don't even know...
you are a man
i am a woman...
the love from a woman
i no longer receive...
it's been awfully hard
to keep up the act...
you don't seem to know me
as i don't know you...
time has been cruel
to both you and i
i yearn for my family
and what once was...
PMS you say? the cause
of my problems...

i thought you understood me
cared about me
treasured me
and knew about my pain...
i guess i don't really know you, Dad
and it doesn't matter now
for you are now placed
with the rest of them
the ones who don't care
the ones who ignore
the ones who are selfish
the causes of my pain...
these are supposed to be
wonderful, happy holidays
i am broken in being
and in spirit...
alone in my grief
you were supposed
to take notice, Dad
how come you didn't?
my tears are flowing
each day reliving the past
how my life without your love
has shaken and broken me inside
i often wonder
what i have done
to be used, discarded
left alone
without a family
without caring people...
alone this Christmas

with my own little unit
you won't be here
with the one who needs you
you've made your plans
and they never include me
funny thing though
i have never done that to you
or the in-laws as you know...
i continue to give
as a daughter full of love
too bad no one can tell me
what i need to hear...
i will wake up once more
my eyes red and swollen
too bad you never noticed, Dad
i am sure you never will...

a private corner

locked in a place
where no one can touch me
curled up in a corner
it's where i will be...
destines for sadness
pain
loneliness
betrayal
i've set myself up
always to fail...
can't touch me
or hold me
i won't let you in
no hope or happiness
left within...
locked up in a place
where no one can touch me
alone in my world
a mighty fortress
to see...
beyond all help
no one to comfort
alone too often
used and discarded
wanting that touch
that love
that friendship
no one to take it
enjoy it and treasure it...

so alone in my corner
all curled up and protected
no one can touch me
hurt me or laugh...
i am protected
my wall surrounds me
i live by myself
free from all harm...

no meaning

no tears left
can't cry anymore
empty shell
wounded
can't heal
broken
identify shattered
too many pieces
can't be fixed
can't be put back
together
go through the motions
like a walking zombie
wear a mask
hide the pain
everything's great
nothing's the matter
a wonderful happy
time of the year...
cannot feel
don't want to feel
the family now broken
the life-chain non-existent
why is this happening?
what did i do?
all i ever wanted
was to be loved
in a family
accepted

cherished...
all i ever wanted
a close knit unit
holidays, special days
events spent together...
whatever happened?
i wish there was an answer...
my life is like a dream
it's hard to comprehend
how much hurt i've had to deal with
the load gets heavier and heavier...
to those who are complete
and have the perfect dream
the closeness
love
acceptance
of a family who
deep down cares...
you are lucky
cherish your moments
the precious times
you celebrate together
i envy you
it's almost like an obsession
something i desperately want
but cannot ever have...
no more meaning
this time of year brings me
sadness
despair
tears and disappointment

i want to move on
but something is in the way
it's time to close the door
and lock it now for good...
throw away the key
to the door
which holds the way to
the pain
disappointment
betrayal
and hurt...

for dad

can't you see
the pain i'm in
the silent tears
that are kept within...
my heart that's broken
my being withered
stupid excuses
always spoken...

you make me feel
like second best
to you it's like
no big deal
tell me one thing
then do another
follow her lead
now it's
all too real...

you've found it better
to be with her
her relatives
her family
yours doesn't matter
not now, not ever...
you do what YOU want to do
no matter it if brings
tears and pain
broken hearts

and empty thoughts...
look into my eyes, Dad
really look deep down
can you see my pain
my sadness
my broken heart
the tears that flow
from the inside now
once again i am alone...
holidays are for families
but where is YOUR family?
don't you care anymore?
are you embarrassed?
or bored?
why am i always left
far behind...
with Mom gone
and you nowhere
to be found
and little brother
at his in-laws
do you not think
about me
even a bit?
i wonder if
my needs are important
or if you just want to
go where the excitement is
forget about me
my family
YOUR family...

you always hurt me, Dad
at this time of year...
i don't know why i
even bother to ask
i ask you each month
and always you say
i don't know yet
maybe or just wait and i'll see
actually you're waiting for a better invitation
one with her family
then you won't have to come
and be with your blood relatives...
for nine years now
since the passing of mom
you've only been with me
two of those holidays...
it's no wonder i'm depressed
so much of the time
i can't depend on you anymore
can't handle the pain
the disappointment
too many tears
aching broken heart...
it doesn't matter
to you anymore
you are set in your ways
not being able to change...
i won't ask you
anymore, Dad
you can spend all your

happy holidays
with her and her relatives...
no more Dad...
i'm done...
i'm tired
of this little old game...
i'm not second best
to anyone
not even you!
i won't ask again...
i won't waste my breath...

thank you, Dad
for making my holidays
so very special each year

the past

do you remember...
the smell of the holidays?
listening to Christmas music
on the record player...
the silver tree
all dressed with blue...
the glass bulbs carefully hung
always the same
the pattern
the blue
the outside lights
the inside lights
the spotlights...
blue...
can you remember?

the snow back then
so much to see
the leaky boots
the soaked mitts
the igloo forts
backyard rinks
and hot chocolate
skating on a pond
tobogganing on a hill
never ever knowing
that the hill
became part of a highway
that now became a memory

do you remember it all?

the Christmas candies
on the table
with the chocolates
the relatives coming over
bringing bundles for you and me
Christmas eve
the snow
the gifts
the visits
the warm feeling...
close your eyes
i can still see it
i am still there...
i want to do back
feel it once more...
Daddy rehearsing
singing for Church
falling asleep to
strains of Oh Holy Night...
waking next morn
to the smell of the turkey
all in the oven
cooking away...
opening gifts
never making a mess
soon as you're finished
quick take them away
can't have a mess
nothing out to display...

the fighting and yelling
can't we please keep them out
other kids have the gifts still
there under the tree
tons of presents for my brother and me
Dad, did you remember
to get a gift for Mom?
how come she buys you
so much stuff
and all you get her is
perfume and slippers?
always the same...
eating at 2 p.m.
then cleanup
just mom and me
no company
no visits
no hugs or kisses
go through the motions
without any emotion
then off to Grandma's
to visit the uncles and aunts
and eight of us cousins...
the relatives of my father
never a mention of mom's family
or relatives...

do you remember
my Christmas's past
some lonely
some happy

being depressed
my family wasn't
the family i wanted
togetherness
with love
being happy
sharing with relatives...

this year i lack the emotion
the excitement
to get involved
maybe my wall is up
can't deal with this season
the past hurts...
the past includes
my mother
no longer alive...
the past bring the truth
my family wasn't perfect
and never ever will be...
decorations everywhere
parties every night...
is this really December?
procrastinating
way behind
buy.buy.buy
can't seem to get it
this year
no drive
no desire
bah humbug i guess...

nothing's the same
too many changes
am tired of my memory
and the Christmases
i left behind...
can't erase the pain
the tears
the loneliness
i hate this time of year
and what it does to me...

the little match that gives great warmth

the little match
that gives great warmth
the little bright beam
that shows me the way
is starting to grow
giving hope
a little smile
a clearer view
reality is within my reach
growing slowly
burning brightly
the solid little light
standing proud
moving with grace
it's tiny but strong
showing the way
giving power and strength
and inner peace...
it lights my way
a faint glimmer
there's hope
not despair...
the little match...
it gives me warmth
and hope
the strength
the courage...
like the light
that continues to burn

never failing
with a purpose...
my life will start
once more
like the match...
my glow
my warmth
will continue to grow
to show the way
to light the path
to live once more
to shine eternally
never flinching or failing
a purpose to live
and face the path...

out in the rain

the winds pick up
the skies turn grey
ominous colours
that are going to stay...

little tiny drops
spitting out from the clouds
one by one
they hit my face
my body
wet and cold...
starting slowly
picking up the pace
quicker they fall
larger each drop
standing there
still and quiet
my whole being
getting wet
this body feeling cold...
soon drenched
even though all alone
i raise my eyes
and look way up...
the clouds
the dark sad clouds
they're crying too...
a flood of tears
raining down from the heavens

a never-ending supply
from cries unheard
voices stifled...

i stand alone
outside
in the rain
far from all the lives
i feel the rain
and all the pain...
outstretching my arms
to the darkening clouds

i yell and scream my rage
the thunder
the heavy drops
and the deafening winds
deaden and silence
the wrath and despair
i so want to release...

life and fairness
love and hate
the rules
so cruelly dictated
destruction and ruin
laid out
for all to see
this world
and what it
was not supposed to be...

thank you for taking my hand

take my hand
walk this road
with me
and never ever
let it go...

promise me
as long
as i breathe
you'll never
ever leave me...

my path
my road
it has been crooked
an uphill battle
all the way...
my being
so broken
so tired
so dejected
now stumbles
and falls
too weak
too frail
to get back up

rapid breathing
becomes shallower

slower
as the strength
the courage
and the will
start to leave
withdraw from the body...

the weight
the struggle
has been borne heavily...
the body
torn and ravaged
betrayed and abandoned
worn and tired
now just rests...
the heartbeat slows
the will to move dies
it is now all
a matter of time...

slowly the eyes
they begin to close
weary and heavy
breathing becomes calmer
slower...
mind closing
body shutting down...

what seems like an eternity
is only a moment in time...
what am i feeling?

is this all real?
what is happening?

strong
yet gentle
firm
and
with purpose
arms and hands
two pairs
are lifting up
this fragile
broken being
giving strength
new courage
some hope
a purpose
to continue,
a desire
to live

and a promise
to take my hand
and walk this
road
my path
alongside me
never
ever letting go...

the struggle

the words
spoken
to no one at all
reveal
just how broken
and shattered
tattered and warn
my mind is tired
thoughts in disarray
sometimes i wonder
why was i born...

the razor
that thought
and the power
it claims...
always there
lurking
waiting
as if like a game...
the struggle
the inner torment
the pros and the cons
give it up or give in
to the power within...
the voice commands strength
bellows low and dark orders
take 'it'
make the first move...

stories of glory
the rush and the wonder
the coolness
the wetness
a bright colour of red...
and a guarantee
to be noticed
and finally heard...

respect me
please hear me,
the words i have spoken
they're important too...
the feelings
my thoughts
the opinions
mine must matter too...
this illness
in full-blown torment
has destroyed
the person within
killed the gifted
the kind, once confident mind...
no longer valued
treasured
or looked up to,
no longer thought of
remembered or
called...
a fraction of the person
i once claimed to be

a sad pathetic
being
is all that i see...

life
it's just a waiting game now...

tonight's misery

it's so cold
hands like ice
breathing laboured
gasping for air
and tears just fall
words scream out
though no one cares
abuse and harm
splattered
against the wall
vicious attack
my whole being flawed
blame and disgust
hatred and lies
a daughter's call
adds to the misery within...

i am slowly withering
dying inside,
and there's nothing left
anymore to hide,
the chore of living
and the pain to survive
the struggle
this act
the character worn
without purpose
or hope
it's difficult to cope

life without desire
exhausted from life
my heart beats steadily
strong and with purpose
my troubled, disturbed mind
died
a long time ago...

what the med websites say to do

ask for help
go see your doctor
instead of
fixing it yourself,
don't stop the pills
no sudden withdrawal,
cause no one
will be there
when you begin the fall...

ask the god
the one who pretends
he's the one
who smiles when you're done,
consult him always
and do what he says
no matter the harm
or lack of concern,
the disrespect shown
the attitude given,
the mentally ill person
continues and searches
tirelessly pleading,
asking and begging
but
no advocate found...

so what does one do?
after one's asked

for the help?
tried to make the contact
system and doctor fail?
who monitors
who cares
who advises the ill
what happens to us
and who the hell cares?

throughout the years

throughout the years
and all of the pain
toughened soul emerged
a fortress built
to end all harm
and keep them far away...

little by little
and through time
i learned to unmask
it all...
how hard it was
no one will know
the effort
the energy expended,
to tell the story
to release the pain
to put my faith
my trust
i gave it all away...

but
like my whole life history
as habit repeats once more
no one has really listened
no one has ever cared...
judged again
just a numbered being...
it took my whole life

to disclose it all...
you didn't fix me
no quick pill you found...
now too tired
and maybe even bored
you wash your hands of me...
you feel defeated
you have given up all hope
i am a waste of breath,
of time
and energy expended...

all of my life
no one has ever listened
no one has ever cared
and no one has heard my cries...

did you know?

did you know?
the nightmares
come so regularly...
did you know?
the anxiety is gaining
the upper hand...
did you know?
the fear is all consuming...
did you know?
the struggle i bear within...

did you know?
i really needed to talk...
did you know?
i wanted to unload it all...
did you know?
how jumbled my thoughts are...
did you know?
i needed to be there...
did you know?
i am trying
as best as i can...

did you know?
i was in deep turmoil
and pain...

Yes,
you probably did know

but you chose
to turn
and look the other way...

you told me once...

you told me once
you'd always be there
we'd ride this road together...
never again
would i have to bear
the pain, the hurt alone...

you told me once
how i could count on you
to trust
to help
to guide
and advise...

you told me once
no matter what,
to call you
when in pain,
if ever a time
when life got tough
you'd always make the time...

you told me once
you'd always be there
and that you really cared,
the talks we shared
the trust we built,
the years of making strides,
bit by bit

moment by moment
time has broken
the fragile trust...
attitude and disregard
it was all a lie...

you told me once
you'd always be there
a play
upon my despair,
clearly now
i see the truth
it's all
in black and white,
no simple fix for this mixed up soul
you failed
both you and i...
abandoned once more
like the others before
i walk towards the door
escape and run
from this moment from hell
alone
i cry
because it was all a lie...

i told you once
i would never ever trust
and that no one could find a fix...
that i wouldn't let you ride my road
or share my heavy load...

You see me
You view me
as giving up on life...
You judged me,
more importantly
You hurt me
but that's okay you see,
i am the one
and the only one
who know all of this before,
i know myself so very well,
You have failed,
You could not help...

mental illness
there is no cure
no quick or easy fix
the system so broken
lives forsaken
and no one seems to care...

Cry

Cry for me
and what i used to be
Cry for my soul
darkened by depression's
heavy toll...
Cry for my being
not worth seeing,
purpose unknown
and never shown,
alive
yet dead,
everyday
full of dread,
how much more
is left to endure?
the fight
the war
a battle within...
Cry for me
because
i can't win,
engulfed
by life's losses
consumed
by darkness
my life,
one big mess,
my mind
in total distress...

Cry with me
for the loss of today
Cry with me
as i grieve the unknown
what was
what is
and what will be...

living in the past

one by one
the memories
live once more
they come alive
the dreams
black and white
now vivid with colour...

close my eyes
and i am there
the past
as real as ever...

snow falling heavily
out past the window
decorated with blue worn lights
the silver tree
and the blue glass balls,
the three sectioned plug-in
circling round and round
giving the tree
hues of green, red, and yellow...

the beautiful music
the harp
the celeste
the voices
the choirs
majestic Christmas sounds

over and over
cherished forever
remembered and loved...

a coffee table
simple,
but filled...
Black Magic chocolates
Christmas assortment
of rock hard candies,
the beloved Torrone
sneaking and sampling them all,
no one looking...
beloved seasonal shows
seen on a black and white TV...
Rudolph the Red-Nosed Reindeer,
The Little Drummer Boy,
with the Vienna Boys choir,
Andy Williams Christmas Specials,
Bing Crosby and White Christmas,
Alistair Sin as Scrooge,
and then midnight mass
Daddy singing
O Holy Night,
and barely keeping
my eyes open
long enough...

going to bed
to the smells of the turkey cooking
and dreaming of

the National Bakery goodies
sitting in the fridge...
no home baking
only mom's shortboard
white as white
delicate little red jam centres...
meatballs cooking
veal, beef, and pork
cooked with love
and attention to tradition...

morning
the dreaded morning
all hell breaking loose
yelling, screaming
fighting
and crying...
Mommy mad at Daddy...
the cold treatment
open the gifts
and don't make a mess
get ride of the wrappings
then take everything
to your bedroom...
no mess in the living room,
don't argue
it's no use,
take them all away....
quiet and behind closed doors
my brother and i
alone with our gifts

no playing together
no laughter ringing through the house...
learning as a child
being and living alone the norm...
the Queen's message
come out of your room
a tradition for all
watch and respect,
Mommy's only link
to her past...

no fancy dishes
the table all set,
the fruit cocktail in bowls
the first course as always
followed quickly by soup
Italian turkey meatball,
the turkey with meat dressing
the corn or asparagus
the mashed potatoes
and the National Bakery's
little sweet treasures...
Daddy's bottle of wine
always red
always ready for sampling

quickly done
the cleanup and more hell
more fights
more words
me and Mommy

and two hours of chores
a woman's job
so i'm told...

at 6:00 p.m.
it's off to Grandma's and Grandpa's
cousins, 8 of us in total
aunts and uncles, 4 of each
so much fun
a happy joyous time
i belong here
i feel connected
loved and admired
treasured by all

i don't realize
how quickly time will go
as i sit amongst family
three generations connected
happy and loved,
nor do i realize just how precious
and sacred through times were
and how much i long
and ache deeply
for my family...

like a whirlwind
life quickly passed by
there is no more connection
death and time
separating the generations

that were...
ignorance and pride
stupidity and anger
they're all my family now
a life filled with regrets
and sadness,
days all alone
to talk in the memories
to live in the past...

my life filled with torment
despair and abuse
emotional bondage
verbal assault
the physical aches
that is what is left...

all i want for Christmas
is
to be loved and accepted
cherished and treasured
respected and cared about
to be whole and alive to trust
and to feel peace...

what am i?

what am i?
by the way i am treated
a used and worn rag
a piece of material
shit on
pissed on
thrown up on
torn and ripped
used to wipe filth
clean up the spills...

what am i?
a smelly torn rag
used over and over again
the gleam is all gone
brightness and sturdiness
well worn...
the rag is all filled
all dirty
and serving no purpose at all...
stained and burned
ready now
to be thrown out...
the rag
no longer of use
purpose fulfilled
reeking with filth
the stench of bodily fluids
stained with blood

excitement and mud...

what am i?
not of much worth
to anyone anymore...
tired of people
and the game they play
hurt
the sting
the pain
second best
i have had enough...

Did you see my tears?

Hey there
did you see my tears?
did you feel my pain?
Where were you
when i needed you most?

How come
my life doesn't matter
to you
or to anyone?
Why is it
that no one cares
to send a card,
say a kind word,
remember a birthday,
i guess it's too hard
to make an effort
an inconvenience
a chore...

unimportant
and of no value
a waste of life and breath
always there
i seem to be,
for all living things...

depending on others
and giving them my soul

brings much sadness
despair and tears...
tired of being mistreated
misused,
my heart forever breaking,
you never saw my tears,
you never felt my pain...

when am i ever going to be 'special'?
important and valued?
loved and cherished,
why do all people
family or friends
see me as a
meaningless being
to be treated
with disregard?
and that anything
ever
to do with 'me'
is such a chore to attend
to phone
to send a loving touch
to say a tender word?

my tears keep falling
my pain, immense
my heart is aching
the loneliness
a burden
the baggage so heavy...

truly alone
the last one standing
a unit destroyed
by death and stupidity
selfishness and pride,
my tears unseen
invisible to you
my pain hidden deeply...
i trust no one
and never will...

a fake party

a party of sorts
of odds and ends,
wear the face
act the part
pretend to be happy
put on a smile...
inside,
a broken heart cries
the river of tears
flow continuously
never ending...
hope for nothing
except nothing
one will never get hurt

try to be social
that's what's expected
always for everyone else...

driven to drink
to mask the pain
another being arises
one of a woman
with no inhibitions
carefree and wild
full of laughter
and smiles,
alcohol a new best friend...

a character unknown
for ever so long
reborn once more,
tobacco and alcohol
enablers of change
transform the broken
wounded character
into someone
no one has seen...

an escape from reality
for just a wee time
playing the part
of the birthday girl
on the outside
through inside,
a dead and dying soul
whose purpose
in life
remains unknown...

mommy

eighteen years
have come and gone
alone i struggle
through
all of the tears...

you took a part of me too
the day you died
life left me also
as i uncontrollably cried...

today i mourn
for what once was
the black and white memories
and the years gone by,
the deep deep longing
for a mother's soft touch,
a hug and a kiss
that i have missed so much...
a relationship shattered
by death's cruel victory
finally setting you completely free,
no more agony
no more pain
your freedom achieved
for all to believe...

left behind
to cope alone

i'm lost
and without purpose...
and i just can't go on...
the pain
the longing
the ache
it's so real,
Mommy
i am crying
i still need you
i still want you
my heart is breaking
are you listening?
my eyes are crying
can't you see?
my tears
they're real
flow freely
without any effort
but
your ears are deaf
your eyes blind
your mind hard
your thoughts cold...

what have you become?
what is your purpose?
where do you fit in
within the constraints
of my troubled mind?

i believe
that you
have caused me
irreparable damage
harm beyond belief
in my quest
however futile,
to become whole
once more...

words spoken
without much thought
disregard for my pain
my past,
the haunting memories
events and actions
they mean nothing
to you...
belittle me
my pathetic thoughts
secretly
laughing inside
ridiculous woman
grow up
wake up
you are an adult,
you stupid stupid fool...

i sought help
and answers,
and i gave in

to the process
reluctantly...
little to realize
i would become
patronized,
my thoughts not recognized
not valued
unimportant
trivial and immature...
to feel belittled
and a poor excuse
for a human being...

there is no answer
there is no help
there never was
and
there never will be...
just as i entered
this world alone,
i face the darkness
of my life
alone...

ready for bed and wide awake

ready for bed
i'm wide awake...
mind pacing
thoughts racing...

ready for bed,
the panic sets in
my day
now ready to begin
and
while others sleep,
i lie awake
and weep...

ready for bed
clearly i see
the waste
this woman
and it is me...

ready for bed
anger and rage
are setting the stage
for what will be
a dark night ahead...

ready for bed
the image is clear
the urge so real

an adrenaline rush
go get the knife
it's no big deal
there's nothing to fear...

ready for bed
the choice all mine
pills or knives
sedate or cut
either way
i'm still in a rut
no rest for the wicked
no sleep for the troubled
my day
just starting
the hell beginning
the dawn awakening
the struggle
sickeningly real

it's time for bed
and i'm wide awake

This is me

Sitting back
reality setting in
my life
my being
all without purpose
and filled with much strife
all messed up
a wasted
pathetic journey
an injured soul
damaged
an existence destroyed
the heart still beats
fragile mind and all feeling
forever deadened
warmth and touch
replaced
cold and indifferent
no reason to care
nothing matters
then and now...

Sitting back
i see so clearly,
my past
black and white
very simple
very sad
a toy for my mother

not a boy for my father
love me, Daddy
being perfect gets noticed
makes Daddy love me,
but that's all i'm good for...

i've lived my life
to make others happy
to fulfill their wants and needs
my existence
my life
my purse meant nothing
my happiness depending
upon their approval...

So now as time goes by
and the years speed ahead
i am left with nothing
life's been hard
and cruel to me
overwhelmed with too much
my dreams destroyed
an image shrinking
day by day, what i am
and what others see in me
and what i feel
all easily hidden,
the clothes,
the makeup,
all a façade...
inside

internally
despair and hopelessness
sad and pathetic

i am dying

becoming deadened

there is no one left
there is nothing more...
betrayal and trust
issues
in the tormented mind...
passed along
abandonment,
the pain
is too much...
where do i look?
what can i go to?
there is no one
two-faced
too busy
a number
without a face
without a being...
the pain
the ache
is so deep
why?
after time and again
the repetition
stabs me over and over
there is nothing left...
no emotion
no desire
there is nothing left
career is gone

no one cares
the harm
the betrayal
the assault
the false accusations
no one has ever cared
the seniority all lost
unbelievable but true
death after death
mom and dad
grandma
my best friend
the drunks
that killed her
and the lives
that were never the same...

apple

God's greatest gifts
His wonderful masterpieces.
Man
and Woman...
what despicable
horrible, hurtful
beings
He has created...
trusting them
loving them
accepting them
now impossible to do...
these wonderful
beautiful masterpieces
have destroyed this being
inside and out...
destiny and truth
now accepted
eyes opened wide
i see what Mankind
is all about...
hatred
despair
selfishness and want
death and dying
broken dreams
unkind words
actions and thoughts...
it is this wonderful

creation
Man and Woman
who have murdered the being
i was
stripped bare
survival
almost impossible
closing down the mind
the body
the spirit
the will to live...
...so tired now...
so tired
of trying to fit in
of trying to play the game of life
of the constant struggle
of the pain that people inflict
of being an intelligent
once caring woman,
who has now been misplaced
and displaced
by life's cruelty
its tragedies
in a fast paced
idiotic
out of control world
filled with His
greatest creations
who really are murderers
assassins...
...i wonder if this was all in His plan

on Creation day?...

Acknowledgements

Heartfelt thanks to the people (my husband especially) who helped me face the darkness within. Thank you for being patient with me. Thank you for your kindness and compassion, and for never judging me. Thank you for your hugs and your presence, even when I tried to push you away. You gave me the courage and strength to do this project. An account was written to my dear children who had their lives turned upside down when their mother became ill. For this tumultuous period in my life, I can only hope that you will one day understand and forgive me, that you will learn to love the person who is your mother.

To Alanna Rusnak Publishing, thank you for your dedication, hard work, and commitment to helping me bring this dream to fruition. You are a gift and so treasured as an author, publisher, and professional.

Finally, I would like to acknowledge God and thank Him for giving me the courage and strength to let the pain come out in the form of this writing project.

About the Author

Denae Turner (not her real name and hidden to protect her identity) is a married, semi-retired woman living in small-town Southwestern Ontario. She is a third generation member of her family suffering from major depression and anxiety.

Look for the next book, *The House on Gollyer* A recollection of life growing up, late 2019.

www.ingramcontent.com/pod-product-compliance
Lightning Source LLC
Chambersburg PA
CBHW060250050426
42448CB00009B/1610